CAREER-BLOCKED:
EDUCATED & UNEMPLOYED

LAURELIS JUSTICE

LAURELIS JUSTICE

Copyright © 2018 Laurelis Justice

All rights reserved.

ISBN: 1724921630
ISBN-13: 978-1724921635

DEDICATION

To my wonderful husband who has watched and supported me, continuing to love and cherish me for better and for worse, for richer and for poorer, in sickness and in health, in good times and in bad.

You are one in seven billion.

LAURELIS JUSTICE

CONTENTS

	Foreword	i
1	Due Diligence & The Dilemma	1
2	SES Bias, Nepotism & Cronyism	3
3	Sexism	5
4	Homophobia	7
5	Ageism	8
6	Disability Bias	9
7	Xenophobia	10
8	Racism	12
9	Religious Bias	14
10	The Why	15
11	The Solution	17

LAURELIS JUSTICE

FOREWORD

So, you finished high school and you decided not to take the work-yourself-up route, the technical skills route, or the just-winging-it route. No, you decided to go to college so that you can go farther up the career ladder, make more money, and gain the knowledge necessary to do well in your chosen field. And that came with a huge price tag, a personal or student loan under the guise of a guaranteed return on investment that will pay you back in unlimited supply. For some people, especially the financially privileged operating in the circle of cronyism and nepotism, it does turn out this way. Those are the people who relish the phrases, "What doesn't kill you makes you stronger," and "Difficulty breeds character," because it is true for them, those with a guarantee. However, for most, it seems that no matter how intelligent you are, no matter how many degrees you earn to prove your intelligence, you just cannot obtain employment in your profession. On top of your student loan debt weighing you down, you have adult responsibilities, regular bills, and now, the pressure from yourself and others to take a job, any job, for any pay just to avoid ensuing financial ruin due to mounting debt and a long period of unemployment which can cause additional problems with finding gainful employment. You did not earn your college degree(s) to work for minimum wage or in a dead end job next to those who chose not to go to college. Yet, that seems to be your future. You are being career-blocked, and there is a reason for that.

1 DUE DILIGENCE & THE DILEMMA

Now, before you start blaming everyone in the world for your well-deserved flops and failings, let's go over some due diligence. First, fresh out of college, unless you have been building verifiable experience, you cannot, reasonably, expect to step into a management position. However, you can, and should, expect an entry-level career position in your field of study with a competitive salary and benefits to match. In other words, your college education is meant to gain you entrance into positions otherwise closed to those without the education and skills that you now possess. It, however, does not gain you an automatic place near the top of the ladder. Climbing the rungs of the career ladder requires both education or knowledge and experience, unless the company promotes based on some other criteria such as longevity or biases (e.g., nepotism, cronyism, etc.)

Second, if you have been in the field a while and have worked your way up while earning your degree, the fact is that the higher level the position, the fewer opportunities available. In effect, getting hired into an executive-level or C-level position is like winning the lottery; there is one CEO at a company that could have hundreds of thousands employees. Consequently, unlike a lottery based on chance, employers rely on another method for choosing their winners which creates your dilemma.

Employers look for reasons *not* to hire you, rather than reasons *to* hire you. This disqualifying process is meant to quickly thin the applicant pool to obtain the *best* candidates, but allows for a great deal of bias under the guise of the applicant being overqualified or not a good fit for the position or for the company culture. Why else would employers require face-to-face or voice interviews before hiring you when your qualifications may be verified through paperwork or contact with previous employers, education institutions, and/or professional or personal references? As long as you are qualified, why is you physical appearance important? Your appearance is important because bias is real and affects everyone, some more than others. The truth is, no matter how noble an employer wants to be, consumers decide from whom they buy. So, employers will choose to employ those who are most aligned with their consumers' culture to gain and maintain business. Moreover, people don't like to feel uncomfortable and people tend to be most comfortable with whom and what they know, people just like them. Yes, this is discrimination and yes, it is illegal to discriminate based on certain protected cultural identifiers including gender, race, age and religion. But you, the applicant, have the burden of proof. Good luck with that! As already established, employers have many canned, legally acceptable, readily available reasons for why they did not hire you.

2 SOCIOECONOMIC STATUS (SES) BIAS, NEPOTISM & CRONYISM

You have done your due diligence; you are not applying for positions that are way outside of your purview or career level. You, now, know employers look to disqualify you, often using several layers and forms of bias. You are not getting interviews or, ultimately, getting hired. So, let us explore some financial biases that may be holding you back.

Have you ever noticed that poverty, crime and violence seem to be concentrated in certain areas? Well, there is a reason for that. By playing on those stereotypes, SES bias allows for discrimination, redlining, under the assumption that people from higher income backgrounds are of better stock and breed, more intelligent and less likely to commit crime. In truth, it is social injustice that creates poverty through marginalization and disenfranchisement which, in turn, tends to breed crime and violence as the impoverished hope to better their situation using the means at their disposal. Marginalization and disenfranchisement are separation to the point of being cutoff completely from resources (e.g., gainful employment, quality healthcare, viable financial institutions, quality housing, grocery stores and healthy foods, quality education, etc.) prevalent in common, more privileged areas. They are forms of oppression that keep people from betterment by either limiting opportunity or removing opportunity, altogether. For instance, checking personal bias, would you date someone who lived in low-income housing? Would you expect that person to pay for your dates? From an employment perspective, have you noticed that areas that have warehousing and lower paying, minimum wage service jobs will be less affluent than areas with corporations and higher paying, salaried office jobs. Have you ever seen a factory or waste facility in a wealthy neighborhood? Even if you land a career opportunity outside your community, you may be priced out of the job due to transportation costs and requirements (e.g., the inability to purchase reliable transportation, auto liability insurance requirement), the cost of car ownership responsibilities like maintenance, the inability to obtain a driver's license, travel time, lack of mass transportation routes or reasonable commute time, something in your background check, or your credit score (e.g., debt-to-income ration, defaults and bankruptcies, liens and judgments, identity theft issues). Depending on how much bias a potential employer holds and exercises, your zip code could very well cost you a job, yes that 5-digit number on your resume and employment application. Other oppressive techniques include requiring unpaid internships (free labor) or requiring extensive (length) or extended (duration) work hours which limit your ability to commute with public transportation or look for other, better opportunities. And while that Equal Employment Opportunity (EEO) questionnaire regarding Section 8 housing, WIC, food stamp vouchers, and other income history qualifiers makes claims of gaining you points for advanced placement, think again. This just may be what human resources needed to disqualify you. Of course, the reason you will get is that you just are not a good fit. So, there will be no EEO complaint for you.

At the other end of the socioeconomic spectrum is favoritism, cronyism and nepotism. These give credence to the old saying, "Birds of a feather flock together." They, likely, grew up together in the same neighborhood, went to the same exclusive ivy-league college, joined the same fraternity or sorority. Their daddies may play golf together at that exclusive country club that requires a certain minimum 7-figure income to join. Even more so, sometimes employers choose who they like rather than who they think can do the job. Regardless, the other guy is in and you are out. Once again, SES bias allows for discrimination under the assumption that money, particularly old money, positively correlates with quality. And since money is the currency of power, those of low SES backgrounds are left powerless and unemployed.

3 SEXISM (CHROMOSOMAL, GENDER BIAS)

No one said that any one thing is the reason you were *not a good fit.* for that company or that job No, there are several categories of discrimination for which you may experience bias. Consider these categories strikethroughs where the more you accumulate, the less likely you will get hired. So, while you may or may not receive a strike for SES challenges, you may build up strikes in other areas like gender. Consequently, ultimately, any discrimination you experience has the potential to snowball into an SES challenge because you can't get hired in your profession.

Historically, males have dominated the workforce so much so that there are still those, both men and women, who believe that woman's work is household work (i.e., cooking, cleaning, child bearing and child rearing). Since women weren't seriously considered for careers, they were paid less and treated as an inconvenience in the workplace, someone men had to accommodate in their workplace and in their world. That considered, is it surprising that women are still paid less even for the same work that men do, that women are still considered an inconvenience where accommodations must be made, that women are still considered intruders in a man's world? It is gender bias that allows discrimination under the assumption that a person's gender, male or female, creates some defect or deficit which prevents or inhibits performance that could otherwise be carried out by the opposite gender. Likewise, those discriminated against are overlooked for employment opportunities, mistreated or harassed as a means to assert power over them, or paid less to show that they are worth less. Other oppressive methods include cutting benefits to eliminate maternity and dependent care, allowing or encouraging an atmosphere for sexual harassment, hiring (or not hiring) on the basis of physical attraction, requiring a special dress code for females (e.g., no open-toe shoes, hosiery mandate, dresses mandate, etc.) and refusing to hire someone with children, of childbearing age, or who is currently pregnant. Consider that the recent

#MeToo movement was decried by many males and females calling it a witch hunt creating an uncomfortable, even hostile workplace with *everyone* having to watch what they say and what they do for fear of being accused of inappropriate behavior. That is correct; finally addressing stewardesses getting slapped on the butt, disparaging and dirty jokes in the workplace, women expected to get the coffee, and quid pro quo, among other things, is what is making *everyone* uncomfortable. And the employer's remedy to this problem is…silencing women or getting them out of the workplace. Sarcastically speaking, that solves the real problem.

4 HOMOPHOBIA (LGBTQ BIAS)

Closely related to sexism (i.e., gender or chromosomal bias), but different in its own right, is bias against those who do not conform to socially acceptable rules for a two-gender society. Like discrimination against males and females, particularly females, bias based on sexual orientation is fueled by assumptions and judgment with regard to how people should and should not behave based on chromosomal make up. One example of LGBTQ bias can be seen in the recent bathroom bill debate on whether or not to provide appropriate facilities (i.e., gender neutral) or allow choice of facility for a non-conforming gender. Another example is apparent in the disregard for female and LGBTQ worth for membership in the U.S. military. I, personally, see both groups holding great potential for intelligence and counterintelligence operations.

Like gender bias, the oppressive nature of homophobia begins when you are required to check the box designating that you are either male or female; those are your only two choices Whichever box you check will set the stage for expectations of dress and style, job performance and potential, and social interaction. If you are male and present too feminine or check the female box, or vice versa, female and present too masculine or check the male box, an assumption will likely be made about your sexual orientation, that you are a gay male, lesbian female, bisexual, transgender, questioning, or confused. You will be an easy target for the *not a good fit* applicant stack. And again, the burden is on you to prove that you did not get the job because you were discriminated against on the basis of your sexual orientation. Given all the possible legally acceptable reasons that an employer can offer up as to why you were not selected (e.g., not a good fit, not qualified, other candidates better qualified, etc.), your chances are slim to none for proving your case. Yes, it *is* very troubling and discouraging.

5 AGEISM

As everybody ages, ageism is a unique form of bias in that, eventually, everyone, except for a lucky few, will experience. The only way to escape discrimination from being too young or too old for employment is through wealth or retirement (by not needing a job) or through entrepreneurship (by being your own boss). Everybody else will have to face a harsh reality that bias really does exist, at least here where assumption are being made about capability based on something that affects 100% of the population because youth and aging are a natural part of life.

Although there is no checkbox for age group on your application, employers date you with many other cues like military service, length of employment history, and education history. Sure, human resources may give you placement points for your military service, but you will lose those points, and then some, when your service dates you as a quinquagenarian (50's), sexagenarian (60's), septuagenarian (70's), or older. Sure, your graduate degree earns you placement points until the hiring official sees that you earned it three or more decades ago. And if you are a child prodigy, you are great until the hiring official sees that you are *just* a child, wet behind the ears, with a doctorate; what experience could you possibly have, kid? Hence, the oppressive nature of ageism is the idea that people hold no worth if they are *too* young or *too* old with the word, too, being totally subjective, left up to hiring officials and their personal biases. Let me ask, how would you feel if a teenaged surgeon walked in your hospital room? How would you feel if a teenaged teacher walked into your child's classroom? What about an octogenarian (80's) surgeon or teacher? The truth is that most people, including employers and their hiring officials, are socialized to associate youth with inexperience and aging with incapacitation, illness and death.

6 DISABILITY BIAS

Similar to the questions about ageism, how would you feel if a one-handed surgeon walked in your hospital room? What about a teacher with a speech impediment, or a mental health professional with a mental health disorder? Would you assume that any of these people would be incapable of performing their duties? Would you *prefer* someone without a disability to perform any of these tasks? Employers and their hiring officials are no different. And after all, employers look to hire people with whom their clients will do business.

Disability status is another unique category in that anyone may become disabled at anytime through illness, accident, or genetics. It may be a mental, physical or emotional issue. It may be developmentally, socially, or environmentally based. Like ageism and sexism, there exists the assumption that people with disabilities are incapable of performing to standard, or at all, rendering them worth less or totally worthless. And because employers look to disqualify as many applicants as they can as soon as possible, those who may require special accommodations (e.g., time off, assistive devices or personnel, adjusted workload or time, etc.) are considered a burden and end up in the *not a good fit* applicant stack. Paradoxically, if you need any accommodations for your disability, you are required to reveal the nature of your disability under the guise of helping the employer prepare for your accommodations. Furthermore, when it comes to disability bias, the disability does not even have to be yours for you to bear the brunt of discrimination. If the hiring official is made aware of a family member's disability, the assumption may be made that your attention, via time off or special accommodations, will be required to act as a caregiver making it your disability by default.

7 XENOPHOBIA, NATIONALISM

When speaking about phobias, like homophobia and xenophobia, it is important to note that hate and anger are based on fear, fear of losing something pleasant (i.e, rights or privileges) or experiencing something unpleasant (i.e., some form of oppression, disenfranchisement, marginalization, etc.). Furthermore, it is important to note that phobias are based in irrational thought; phobias lack logical reasoning with people unable to coherently explain and support why they feel the way they do. Reasoning is based on erroneous data or outdated, skewed research usually found in demagoguery. For instance, many nationalists argue that immigrants take all the jobs due to Affirmative Action and overtax and abuse the system meant for taxpaying citizens. These arguments assume that immigrants don't pay taxes, but are receiving some form of monetary government assistance; and that immigrants are not registered citizens. While *some* of this may be true for *some* immigrants, immigrants cannot be employed, legally, without paying taxes. So, the problem is with the government and employers (not the immigrants) for giving away assistance to non-citizens and not collecting taxes. Second, immigrants can never pay taxes if employers discriminate against them by not hiring them.

That said, xenophobia is bias against people from other nations, hence the interchangeable term nationalism. Nationalism is akin to racism in that most countries are made up of one ethnicity (e.g., Irish from Ireland, Scottish from Scotland, Mexicans from Mexico, etc.) where those indigenous discriminate against newcomers, but different in that other countries, like America, are made up of people of many ethnic backgrounds with discrimination taking place against newcomers as well as racial minority groups who were born in the country (e.g., African-Americans, Cuban-Americans, Muslim-Americans, etc.). Employers may avoid or cut short interviews when speaking to someone with a thick accent, or avoid interviewing applicants requiring a work visa. Employers may take cues from applications and resumes like your first or last name, zip code, or education history to identify your indigenous heritage. At a company that supports nationalism, Juan is less likely to get a job over John. Likewise, Juan is more likely to be considered for blue collar work; whereas, John would be considered for white collar employment. Disgusting, but true, this is how nationalism works. Employers make assumptions about your intelligence, capabilities, and social skills. You are marginalized and, ultimately, disenfranchised based on your nationality and/or indigenous heritage.

8 RACISM (ETHNIC BIAS)

As previously mentioned, nationalism and racism are closely aligned. As such, this section may be seen as a subcategory of nationalism and xenophobia. For clarification, nationalism is a distorted form of extreme patriotism where outsiders, immigrants, are considered a threat to the indigenous inhabitants' way of life. Racism is based on the belief that people of different ethnic origins have different capabilities. Race is a social construct created in an attempt to separate people from different ethnic origins into categories for sociopolitical and socioeconomic purposes. Ethnicity is based on customs, traditions and indigenous heritage, not skin color.

In my time, and for a long time, there were two or three choices on an employment application when it came to race, White or Black, and later, Other. As simple as this may have been for Europeans to check White, this had to have been perplexing and frustrating for Asians, Latinos, and bi-racial people, although bi-racial people were often given a choice or forced to check Black. Some time in the 90's, a more inclusive re-classification allowed a further break down of the three categories including the option to not identify. As a White person, have you ever elected not to identify? No, of coarse you checked White because it is highly unlikely that anyone would hide a cultural identifier when it gains them privilege. Similarly, a male wouldn't elect to not identify. So, in essence, electing not to identify tells your employer that you are not in a privileged, preferred group (i.e., White, male, heterosexual, etc.). In other words, checking any boxes other than White, male, and heterosexual puts you in danger of discrimination, regardless of Affirmative Action/EEOC guidelines because, as mentioned many time before, you have the burden of proof in a discrimination claim and employers have many legally acceptable, generic, canned responses for why they chose to pass on you, the applicant. Besides the EEO questionnaire, employers may used an applicant's name to identify race, whereby Yetunde, Mufasa and Shameka are less likely to be hired over Melanie, Michael, and Sally. Other than choosing not to hire an applicant at all, employers that practice racism may also avoid hiring ethnic minorities for higher level positions relegating them to dead end, low-level, low-paying, and sometimes even hazardous, service positions reminiscent of slave labor. Other oppressive methods used to disenfranchise ethnic, and religious, minorities may include shunning or banning cultural practices and attire (e.g., dashiki, saree, turban, burqa, yarmulke, etc.), including hairstyles (e.g., afro, braids, payots, natural hairstyles). In turn, these practices perpetuate socioeconomic problems in minority communities. On a side note, because many people tend to get confused with the usage of the terms minority and majority, minority status is based on power dynamics, historical oppression of a cultural group, rather than population. Minority groups have been historically discriminated against perpetuating an underprivileged, disempowered state and may outnumber the privileged, the people with money and power.

9 RELIGIOUS BIAS

Often intersecting with ethnic and gender bias, religious bias is an attack on a person's belief system and practices as they relate to existence, purpose, and morality. In America, if you are not Christian, you are susceptible to religious bias. Although religion is not something that is usually as readily known as other cultural identifiers, you cue employers through mandatory application data, *optional* EEO data, and personal details like requests for specific days off and the reason for your request.

Religion is a major point of contention because people build their entire lives on, and around, their belief, or disbelief, in a Creator. Furthermore, depending on the denomination, some religious practices encourage recruitment into their group and/or shunning of others outside their religious group. As such, religion is supposed to be one of those protected cultural items under the Constitution and enforced by the EEOC. Unfortunately, people tend to miss the concepts of marginalization and disenfranchisement in choosing to celebrate one religion's holy days with paid time off or festivities, while ignoring others'. Celebrating Christian holidays (e.g., Christmas, Easter, etc,), but not Muslim, Jewish, or other non-Christian holidays is the equivalent of celebrating some employees' birthdays, but not others'. And just because it is tradition, the way things have always been, does not make it any less discriminatory or hurtful to those being excluded. Moreover, employers choosing to forego all holidays, a form of punishment rather than remediation, instead of choosing to take an inclusive approach, breed an atmosphere of anger, resentment and contempt among their employees. As a result, as in the case of any minority issue, employers and employees would rather avoid feeling uncomfortable by keeping out those who bring up feelings of discomfort, maintaining the status quo. In short, Becky is hired and Mohammed is not a good fit for the company culture.

10 THE WHY

Everyone, everyone wants to feel a sense of accomplishment, progress towards fulfilling a purpose. Anytime you are forced to check the box, "I don't work," you get a subliminal message shaming you, telling you, not that you are unemployed but, that you are broken, worthless. This shaming is perpetuated through the media announcing that there are plenty, of job openings against a high unemployment rate. This shaming is perpetuated whenever you receive side-eye for collecting your unemployment insurance that you paid for through an automatic employment tax that you can only withdraw if you've paid your money into that account. Surely, you must be unemployed at your own will with all the job openings. You must want to sit at home and live off unemployment. You couldn't possibly be discriminated against with affirmative action and EEOC protections. You could find a job if you wanted one. Your inability to find work is an excuse to not work. Does this sound familiar? That's because it's politics!

Capitalism works by selling something, or someone, for more than what you paid so that you earn a profit. If groups of people are devalued and made to believe they are worth less, or worthless, employers are able to pay those groups less. Career-blocking is a term I coined to demonstrate how minorities have their career paths obstructed, regardless of their education and skills, forcing them into lower labor and slave labor. Although redlining and slave labor are not new concepts, what was introduced was the belief that there are protections against such practices through the eradication of Black Codes which criminalized African-Americans for unemployment making it more difficult to obtain gainful employment, the institution of Civil Rights laws including minimum wage which some employers still are able to circumvent with wages plus tips pay structure, Affirmative Action and the Equal Employment Act which ended up bureaucratic checkboxes that create animosity under the guise that minorities receive some employable advantage rather than offering protection to minorities who continuously face employment discrimination, and federal student aid programs which ended up slavery via indebtedness, similar to sharecropping or owing the company store, rather than an equal educational opportunity for equal career opportunities and advancement. So, the sociopolitical and socioeconomic game never changed, only how the game is played. There is nothing wrong with you. It is not you. Career-blocking is political.

11 THE SOLUTION

The world is against you, but you must live in it and be a part of it. So what do you do? Well, negativity is never a positive; that's why it's called negativity. So, forget the so-called pep talks that encourage consistently and constantly taking a beat down from people telling you that you are not qualified, not good enough. What doesn't kill you doesn't make you stronger; it leaves wounds that fester or turn into scars. Oppression needs an outlet and it *will* find an outlet, preferably a positive one.

Currently, money is the currency of power. In essence, money buys you freedom and some protection from oppression. Enjoy life, but save what you can whenever you can. Your potential for indebtedness is equal to your current savings and your personal income less your current and future responsibilities. In other words, underestimate your income while overestimating your expenses because you can only count on what you have; don't count your eggs before they hatch because your current income may not be indicative of future earnings, and unexpected expenses will occur.

As education seems to be moving towards a socialized approach, free for all for the betterment of society, enjoy a free education that can lead you into entrepreneurial opportunities, whether technical school or college. If you work for yourself, you are your own boss, as long as you avoid indebtedness. Remember, any form of debt is slavery. Education, if not free, is an unsecured investment with all the risks. Some careers to consider are those that people cannot do without; if you were starting your own civilization, what skills would you want your people to have? Consider healthcare and medicine, auto mechanics and restoration, construction and home repair, tailoring and sewing, HVAC and plumbing, appliance repair, agriculture, blacksmithing and hardware, merchandising supplies, and goods and veterinary medicine. Above all, consider that education may come at a price, but wisdom, the ability to apply knowledge with discernment, is priceless. Life isn't about money or power, but purpose. So, find out what it is you *really* want to do, then find a way to do it. Don't give up and don't settle; there's more than one way to pet a cat...Yes, I know that's not the saying. Also, when you get to where you want to be, reach back and help others; network to help break the wheel of oppression.

Watch your own bias because you, and people like you, one day, may be the employer. I, recently, saw a commercial where a politician touted selling books door-to-door to pay for her college education, as if anyone who wanted to go college could do the same thing. Knowing your own biases requires you to acknowledge that what you look like (e.g., ethnicity, gender, age, skin color, physique, attractiveness, etc.) will effect, and determine in most cases, whether or not people will, in this instance, buy from you, in other instances, hire you. People, employers, pretend to discriminate based on education level, but even when that level is attained, surpassed, people, employers will find some other thing wrong with you. An easy formula for employers should be Employed=Ability/Bias; can the person do the job regardless of personal biases? Were you satisfied that the applicant was qualified before the interview? Is the interview only to further verify or clarify qualifications? Before you disqualify an applicant, ask why the applicant isn't a good fit? What does that mean? Is it really a negative that the applicant is overqualified and can the applicant be promoted to another position once hired? Ultimately, people, employers have to ask if employment is a privilege or a requirement? If employment is a privilege, why shame people for lack of income, lack of employment, drawing on their unemployment? If employment is a requirement, why deny people the right to work in their profession, and then shame them for being relegated to another occupation, for being unemployed for lack of work within their profession, and/or for their level of income? We, all, hold some bias and thus, must actively check to identify them and avoid inflicting them on others or they will spread like a communicable disease. Everyone has worth and purpose which are not determined by any other person or group of people. However, until people stop associating employment with worth, avoid asking people what they do for a living; it can be emasculating and demeaning for those who have been already wounded by oppression. Finally, consider moving to another city, state, or more likely, another country where your education and skills are valued over oppressive sociopolitical games.

ABOUT THE AUTHOR

Raised by an educator and experiencing no real educational difficulties in school, I didn't really give much thought to what I would do after high school; college was a given. I completed my degree with honors in less than four years anticipating my life and career as a college-educated lady. I thought I did everything right, studied an area of interest, graduated with honors, and applied for jobs in my field, but received no job offers. So, I took temporary jobs outside of my field of study, ended up going to graduate school in a complementary area of study, but still received no real career offers. After feeling worth less, and eventually worthless, from taking low-wage jobs sitting next to people who never considered college and who didn't incur my college debt, I read a lot, researched a lot, and listened a lot. And then, I wrote this book.

###

Davy2Jones

Workplace harassment defined
The business case for workplace harassment awareness and prevention
Proven strategies to maintain awareness of and prevent workplace harassment
2016 Select Task Force Report on the Study of Harassment in the Workplace
Bystander intervention training

Workplace Harassment
Awareness and Prevention